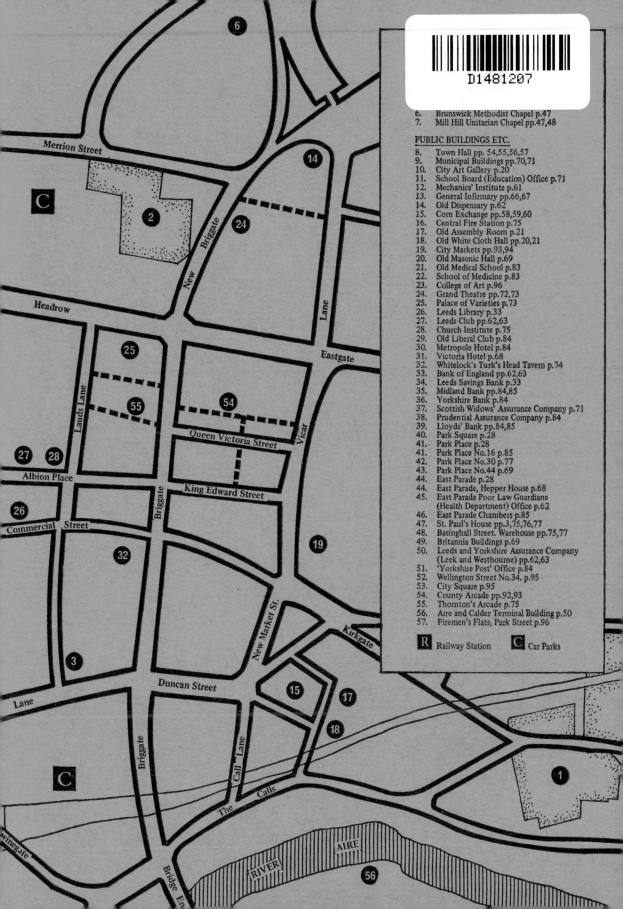

R Railway Station   C Car Parks

D1481207

Merrion Street

C

Headrow

New Briggate

Lane

Eastgate

Lauds Lane

Queen Victoria Street

Vicar

Albion Place

Briggate

King Edward Street

Commercial Street

New Market St.

Kirkgate

Duncan Street

Lane

Briggate

Call Lane

The Calls

C

winegate

Bridge En

RIVER AIRE

HISTORIC ARCHITECTURE
OF LEEDS

Frontispiece. *Church of St. John the Baptist, Adel. Bronze Knocker*

HISTORIC ARCHITECTURE OF LEEDS

by
Derek Linstrum

Sponsored by
LEEDS CIVIC TRUST

ORIEL PRESS

ACKNOWLEDGEMENTS

I am grateful to all the owners and tenants of buildings, vicars of churches, and interested passers-by who have gone out of their way to help me during my many walks round the city. If any owners are surprised to find their property displayed in these pages I hope that they will forgive me for having omitted to seek their permission, and take the inclusion as a compliment. So many people have given me information that I cannot possibly name them all, but I would like to thank the City Librarian's staff particularly for their help. Ursula Clark of Oriel Press and I took many of the photographs especially, but I am grateful for permission to use the illustrations by:-

Peter Burton, John Edenbrow, the Controller H.M.S.O., the Director of Leeds City Art Gallery and Templenewsam, Leeds City Engineer, Leeds City Librarian, Alan Luty, the Royal Institute of British Architects, the Thoresby Society and the Yorkshire Post. My final and deepest gratitude must be reserved for the Council of the Leeds Civic Trust which has so generously subsidised the publication of this book.

Title Page. St. Paul's House, Park Square, 1878. Detail of Doorway

Published by
ORIEL PRESS LIMITED
at 27 Ridley Place, Newcastle upon Tyne NE1 8LH
Text set by City Engraving Company (Hull) Limited,
17 Ryde Avenue, Hull
Printed by Lund Humphries
Bradford

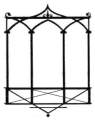

by JOHN BETJEMAN

This book may be an eye-opener to many who live in Leeds. It should be an inducement to those who have not been to the City to come and visit it. It is the work of a native of Leeds who knows and loves the place.

Leeds is too often dismissed as newish, grimy and industrial. It has a history which goes back in stone to the middle ages. It was founded on the wool trade which the monks started at Kirkstall. Looking through these pages one can see the gradual growth of an English provincial town, with some exceptionally grand 17th century work. Then there was an 18th century local brick Georgian style such as still survives in Park Square. But the real flowering of the City of Leeds was in the 19th century. This started with the flax mills, like that remarkable building in the Egyptian style, Marshall's Mills. Leeds prospered with the cloth trade and finally branched into engineering. No city of the North of England has so fine a swagger in the way of 19th and early 20th century architecture as Leeds, whether it is in churches, mills, shops or private houses, stone, brick or terra-cotta. Everybody knows about Cuthbert Brodrick's superb Town Hall of Leeds, but who knows about Corson and Ambler, local Leeds architects, every bit as virile and original in their way as was Brodrick ? Leeds was so important a City, that the big men from London came and did their best here. Sir Gilbert Scott's Infirmary, Waterhouse's University and Banks, Bodley's St. Matthew's and St. Edward's, Pearson's St. Michael's, Headingley — and as good as all these is St. Bartholomew's, Armley, by a local man.

At the end of the 19th century and the beginning of this, Leeds burst into a riot of commercial art nouveau, typified by the Arcades, which are such a feature of the City, by Frank Matcham, who designed the County Arcade, and Leeming and Leeming who did the Markets.

Leeds may look dark on the outside, but inside it is full of colour and warmth. The comparatively unpretentious exterior of the Grand Theatre and the Arcades themselves outside may not lead you to expect the riches you find once you are under cover. Like all northern cities, Leeds depends on outline against the sky for its exterior effects. This was recognized early by the medieval architects, and in the beginning of the last century by Chantrell in his exterior of the Parish Church. Domes and spires and towers have adorned Leeds skyline since. Always there are outside the moors.

I had the pleasure of spending a hot August in Leeds making a film. Even in August I found it a good, lively City to live in, with theatres going on, cinemas, variety, and, outside, parks and country, and between the parks and the country, graceful suburbs, leafy and varied. The work took me into all parts of the City and out into the suburbs. It took me to Roundhay Park and Templenewsam, it sent me back to the centre of Leeds, pleased to be there in the heart of things where Alfred Drury's nude ladies electrify the City Square. The individuality of Leeds is expressed in its buildings, private mansions and public halls and churches. A record like this is invaluable. If Leeds loses these buildings, it might just as well be a bit of that international nothingness which is turning so many of our historic and industrial cities into cheap imitations of America.

What impresses me about this book is its sense of proportion. Each century is given due weight up to 1914, which is, one might say, the watershed of one kind of life.

It was a curious chance of history that linked the 19th century, the time when new industries and wealth were transforming Leeds into an important provincial city, with the remote time before the Norman invasion. When the old parish church of St. Peter was being demolished in 1838 the architect, Robert Chantrell, noticed that some old carved stones had been built into the medieval fabric. Several of them were found to form the greater part of a sculptured shaft which was put together and finally placed in Chantrell's new parish church as evidence of the antiquity of the site.

The style of the interlaced decoration separating the representations of the four Evangelists suggests that the shaft was erected as a monument in the 10th or 11th century, and it confirms the Domesday Book record that there was already a church in the area in 1086.

The history of Leeds before this date is obscure. It was possibly a Roman settlement at the first place above the marshes of the Vale of York where the Aire could be forded, but the main Roman road crossed the river about ten miles south-west. There are no remains of earlier work than the sculptured shaft although there are references in Bede to the setting up of a new royal seat within the *regio* of Loidis in the 7th century, and to an old stone altar in 'the monastery that lies in Elmete Wood', which momentarily dispel the obscurity surrounding the pre-Norman settlement.

Possibly the church of St. Peter was built on the site of this altar and so became the nucleus of a hamlet on the north bank of the Aire, surrounded by other hamlets which later became the medieval parish of Leeds.

Left. Parish Church of St. Peter.
Anglo-Saxon Cross
Page 7. Kirkstall Abbey. North Transept

8   Norman Settlement

View from South-East

West Doorway

The remoteness of Kirkstall in the Aire valley accorded with the strict Cistercian rule of abstinence from all worldly distractions, and in this isolated place the great bare monastic buildings were erected in the two or three decades following the foundation of the abbey in 1152; they were completed in a short time and hardly altered afterwards until the dissolution in 1540.

The monks at Kirkstall came from Fountains Abbey and, in their new building, they followed the same Cistercian pattern; the details were simple and largely undecorated but although the windows and doorways had the familiar round Norman heads the arches of the vaulting were pointed. The mouldings and capitals were consistent with the transitional period when the Norman form of construction was changing to the Gothic. In the 15th century the great east window was substituted for the smaller Norman pattern and in the following century, shortly before the dissolution, the tower over the crossing was increased in height.

At about the time of the abbey's foundation a small church was built at Adel, three miles north of Kirkstall. It had a simple plan but in spirit it was a great contrast to Kirkstall. There was no Cistercian restraint and the south porch and chancel arch were sumptuously decorated with bands of zig-zag patterns and animal heads. The capitals were carved with animals and with representations of Christ's baptism and crucifixion. More heads were carved in the corbel-frieze along the sides and round the gable, and the great bronze door-ring (frontispiece) showed the swallowing of a man by an open-mouthed monster—a warning of Man's possible fate on the Day of Judgement. Above the south doorway the gable was filled with panels representing the four Evangelists and Christ in Majesty.

Norman Settlement

9

Church of St. John the Baptist, Adel, mid 12th Century

Above Right. Part of carving on South Doorway

Right. Detail of Chancel Arch

House in Briggate, probably late 16th Century (demolished)

The medieval town grew round three distinct centres—the park and mills of the Royal Manor on the west, the road (Briggate) leading from the bridge over the Aire, and the hamlet round the church of St. Peter on the east. There had been a bridge across the river since at least 1372 and it was there that the cloth market was held until 1648, 'the Cloths being laid upon the Battlements of the Bridge and upon benches below.' The shops and houses of the merchants were built in Briggate and in the courts and yards which opened off it; the medieval layout can still be seen but almost all the contemporary buildings have been replaced. The last of the medieval frontages in Briggate showed the type and scale of the original buildings although its timber framework had been covered with plaster.

The Leeds Mill, the oldest and largest of the industrial sites on the riverside, recorded in the Domesday Book, was the most lucrative part of the Royal Manor. The residents in the town were compelled to have their corn, grain and malt ground at the mill and pay the leaseholder for the privilege, a monopoly which continued until 1839. The only reminder of this large group of buildings is a 19th century stone panel inscribed KINGS MILLS built into the wall of the wharf on the north bank of the river.

The church of St. Peter was the single building of note in the medieval town; it was a mixture of work from the 14th to the 16th centuries, not unlike the present church in size but quite dissimilar in its internal arrangement. Although none of the medieval fabric was retained in the 19th century rebuilding the old font was preserved and some of the glass and a number of monuments were re-used in the new church.

Parish Church of St. Peter. Font late 16th Century (?) (Cover late 17th Century)

Medieval

ST. MARY'S CHURCH, WHITKIRK

The only medieval church left inside the city is at Whitkirk, where an early (possibly 11th century) stone building which gave its name to the district, was replaced by the present largely 15th century church. Externally it is a low, wide building with a peculiarly Yorkshire corbelled parapet round the sturdy tower and the body of the church. Although it was restored in 1855-6 and the chancel was lengthened by G. F. Bodley in 1901, it still retains a good deal of the medieval fabric but the original furnishings have all been replaced. The south chapel was founded as a chantry in 1448-9 and the alabaster tomb of Sir Robert Scargill and his wife was erected there in the mid-16th century. But it is the later monuments, particularly of the owners of the nearby Templenewsam, that give the church its distinction although their magnificence cannot overshadow in interest the memorial to the locally born John Smeaton, the builder of the third Eddystone lighthouse.

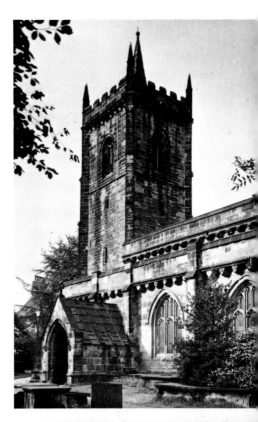

Above. Exterior from North-West

Below right. South-East Chapel

Below. Tomb of the Scargills

ST. JOHN'S CHURCH, BRIGGATE

St. John's was begun in 1631 and consecrated three years later, yet from the outside it could be mistaken for a church of the late 15th century. The strength of the local building traditions and the tenuous communications with London caused a time lag of a generation or two in the adoption of new architectural ideas in the north.

The interior of the twin-naved church was filled with elaborately carved pews, screens and a pulpit which is similar in form and decoration to the contemporary example from Templenewsam. The richly carved decoration and the plasterwork followed the late 16th century fashion derived from the Low Countries but there is no suggestion of the end of a tradition; it is full of vigour and invention.

The original layout of the interior was altered in the 19th century when the building was restored by Norman Shaw. The intention in 1865 was that it should be demolished but Shaw, seconded by Giles Gilbert Scott who said that 'no other town in England can produce a parallel' prevailed on the Bishop to allow the building to be restored, not demolished. In spite of Shaw's praise of the building the restoration was drastic and much of the carving was removed, but amends were made later in the century when all the woodwork that had survived was replaced.

The Pulpit

Detail of Carved Screen

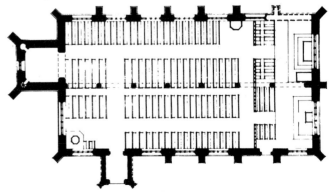

ST. JOHN'S CHURCH, BRIGGATE

The traditional methods of house building changed slowly in Yorkshire. Farm houses continued to be built of stone with mullioned windows and carved lintels over the doors; in the houses of the merchants and local gentry the doorway was usually the only part of the facade which showed the fashion for Classical details, as in Weetwood Hall's typical porch with widely spaced Ionic columns and Knostrop Old Hall's crudely carved door pilasters and balusters in the parapet. In the town, some of the interiors were almost as richly decorated with woodwork as St. John's Church, or with elaborately plastered ceilings as in Weetwood Hall. Almost at the end of the century, Austhorpe Hall was built to an unusually sophisticated design with stone quoins contrasting with the brickwork, a hipped roof instead of the traditional gable, and a Baroque doorway.

Above. Knostrop Old Hall, early 17th Century (demolished). From photograph c.1870

Centre and Below right. Weetwood Hall 1625. Ceiling in Entrance Hall and Doorway

Below. Austhorpe Hall 1694

ST. MARY'S CHURCH, WHITKIRK
Irwin Monument 1697 by John van Nost

TEMPLE NEWSAM

The manor of Newsam, recorded in the Domesday Book, passed through many owners' hands until it was acquired by Sir Arthur Ingram in 1622. In the early 16th century a house had been built by Thomas, Lord Darcy, part of which was retained in the centre of the new mansion. The brickwork and the bay windows on the west side of the present building remain from Darcy's time but the new work transformed it into a typical great house of the Jacobean period. The plan was conservatively E-shaped and the building showed no sign of Inigo Jones's revolutionary ideas derived from the writings and practice of Andrea Palladio; the Long Gallery and the screened entrance hall in the south wing followed the pattern of Elizabethan and early Jacobean houses. The entrance porch incorporated Classical columns but they were the coarse Flemish version, not in the least in accordance with the correct Italian design. Round the top of the house Sir Arthur declared his piety and loyalty in carved letters eighteen inches high: ALL GLORY AND PRAISE BE GIVEN TO GOD THE FATHER THE SON AND HOLY GHOST ON HIGH PEACE ON EARTH GOOD WILL TOWARDS MEN HONOUR AND TRUE ALLEGIANCE TO OUR GRACIOUS KING LOVING AFFECTION AMONGST HIS SUBJECTS HEALTH AND PLENTY BE WITHIN THIS HOUSE.

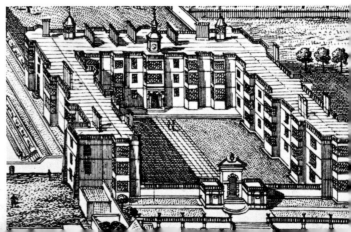

Seventeenth Century

West Front. Centre 16th Century, extended 1622 by Sir Arthur Ingram

Page 16. Entrance Porch and Engraving 1699 by J. Kip after drawing by Leonard Knyff

Late 17th Century Glass from Chapel probably by Henry Gyles

The house was almost entirely remodelled in the 18th century but there are sufficient relics of the chapel in the north wing to suggest that the inside of the house was as conservative as the outside. The pulpit was vigorously carved by Thomas Ventris with geometrical patterns, squat pilasters and ornate friezes; the walls were decorated with painted panels of Old Testament figures by John Carleton and the windows were filled with coloured glass, armorial rather than ecclesiastical, at different times up to the end of the 17th century.

Pulpit from Chapel c.1636 by Thomas Ventris jnr. (now in Methodist Chapel, Halton)

Long Gallery. Remodelled 1738-45

Ceiling of Library (now Chapel) 1740-45

Eighteenth Century

There was not sufficient work of importance in Leeds to encourage the development of a local school of craftsmen and when Henry, 7th Lord Irwin, began to remodel Templenewsam in 1738 in an unlikely attempt to Palladianize the great 17th century house he had to look to York for his craftsmen. He employed Thomas Perritt and Joseph Rose to decorate the ceilings in the new Saloon and Library, which he made out of the old Long Gallery. The elaborately carved doorcases were probably the work of Richard Fisher, another notable York craftsman. As far as possible, Palladian examples were followed; the two monumental chimney pieces in the Saloon were based on designs by William Kent and the gate piers were copied from those at Chiswick, the home of Lord Burlington. The main rooms in the west wing were redecorated at about the same time and the external appearance of the house was changed by the substitution of sliding sash windows for the 17th century casements, and by the building of a large pedimented stable block round a courtyard north of the house.

At the end of the century further alterations were made by the widow of the 9th Viscount. Lancelot "Capability" Brown landscaped the park in the late '60's and at the same time he was consulted about the rebuilding of the south wing; John Carr and Robert Adam were later asked to prepare designs but finally, in 1796, the wing was altered and refaced by a Mr. Johnson in a style which was a conscious attempt to work in the alien manner of Sir Arthur Ingram's original house. The Georgian alterations were completed in the early 1820's when a Chinese wallpaper, the gift of the Prince Regent to Lady Hertford (who had inherited Templenewsam in 1807) was hung in the small Drawing Room next to the Great Hall.

Long Gallery. Fireplace carved by Richard Fisher
Wallpaper in Chinese Drawing Room

Moot Hall, Briggate, altered 1710 (demolished).
Engraved by Charles Heath after Thomas Taylor c.1825
(Statue of Queen Anne now in City Art Gallery)

Left. White Cloth Hall. Cupola 1775

The Moot Hall, a 17th century building which was extended and partly rebuilt in 1710, stood prominently in the centre of Briggate. It was typical of a provincial mason's work based on architectural fashion at the turn of the century; the end wall was decorated with a pair of giant pilasters, an open pedimented gable and a cupola. A Baroque niche was set up over the twin arches in 1713 to be filled with a statue of Queen Anne by Andrew Carpenter who supplied lead figures to Castle Howard, Wrest Park and other important houses.

In 1711 a White Cloth Hall was built in the Calls, only to be replaced in 1775 by its successor, the facade of which still survives in Crown Street. Down one side an Assembly Room was built in the same year, of which some fragments of the original decoration and a large Palladian window remain in their changed context.

When it was proposed in 1767 to build an Infirmary the leading Yorkshire architect, John Carr, was commissioned to make the design. The building, which was opened in 1771, was a plain brick Palladian design with a central pedimented bay and end pavilions. In appearance it was not unlike a country house of the period, its ornamentation confined to a neat Tuscan doorway and three overarched Palladian windows.

Assembly Room. Facade 1775

Infirmary 1770-71 (demolished). Engraved 1771 by Wilkinson

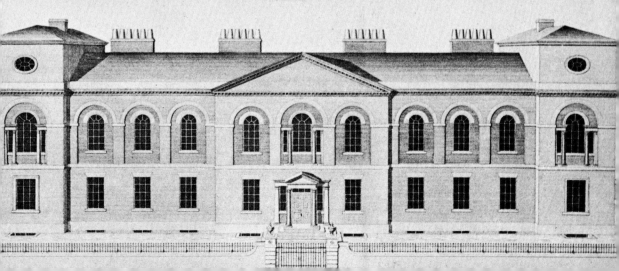

HOLY TRINITY CHURCH, BOAR LANE, 1722-26
Architect William Halfpenny

Carving
in Apse

Pew End
1883-6
by T. Winn

HOLY TRINITY CHURCH, BOAR LANE, 1722-26
Architect William Halfpenny

The most important of the century's architectural additions to the town was Holy Trinity Church in Boar Lane. It was designed in 1722 or 1723 by William Halfpenny (a carpenter from Twickenham whose real name was Michael Hoare), who is remembered for his builders' pattern-books rather than for his buildings. The church was completed in 1726, and externally it was a mixture of the style of the short-lived English Baroque and the new Palladianism that was changing English architecture. The real door on the left of the south front was confusingly balanced, for the sake of symmetry, by a false door on the right. The present tower, designed in 1841 to replace the earlier spire which was damaged in a storm, was an exercise in the Wren-Gibbs manner by R. D. Chantrell. Halfpenny's original design (reproduced in 1724 in Thoresby's 'Vicaria Leodiensis') suggests that the original intention was to have a squat tower only, but the church and the Leeds skyline were enhanced by the 19th century addition. Although there have been several alterations inside the building the present appearance is a fine example of the dignified form of design based on a Roman basilica which was considered appropriate for an ecclesiastical building in the late 17th and early 18th centuries. The pulpit and the decoration of the chancel apse are original but the richly decorated pew ends were a late 19th century addition.

Part of Facade to Boar Lane

Tower 1841 added by R.D. Chantrell

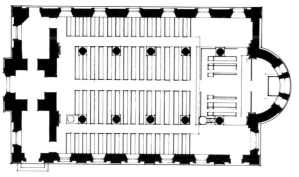

Clough House, Chapel Allerton,
early 18th Century

Dial House, Halton, 1755

About 1725 John Cossins drew the first town map and decorated it with the facades of the houses of the leading citizens. The last was demolished in 1968 but there are several large houses outside the area of the town as Cossins drew it. At that time the churches of St. Peter and St. John were on the fringe of the town, and Holy Trinity was within sight of the surrounding fields and trees.

Fifty years later it had expanded very little and was still surrounded by open country and villages in which some handsome houses had been built. Some were well-proportioned, plain brick buildings with little ornament; others had pediments and decorative stone doorways.

Bischoff House, Hartley Hill, c.1725 (demolished). Facade and Staircase

Gledhow Hall. Built or altered 1766-67 by John Carr

RED HALL, SHADWELL

Above. House refaced late 18th Century
Left. Staircase c.1730
Below. Stables. Pleasant example of Georgian vernacular

Page 27.
Above. Denison Hall, Hanover Square, 1786
Below left. Rosemount, Chapel Allerton, late 18th Century
Below right. Claremont, Clarendon Road, late 18th Century, altered 1865. (Now Headquarters of Leeds Civic Trust, Yorkshire Archaeological Society and Thoresby Society)

Park Square, started 1788

Blenheim Terrace, started 1831 but built in the 18th Century tradition

As in almost all towns the good-class residential area developed on the west side; in 1767 building started in Park Row, in 1776 in South Parade, in 1778 in Park Place and in East Parade from 1785. Most of these streets were rebuilt as the commercial centre expanded in the 19th century although there are still some remains of the original houses. From 1788 onwards Park Square was developed, and this still retains the character of an 18th century town square in spite of the buildings on the south side. Attempts to lay out regularly planned residential areas in other parts of the town such as Queen Square and the later Hanover, Woodhouse and Blenheim Squares largely failed, although in all of them there are pleasant examples of 18th and early 19th century town houses. The industrial buildings were growing up all around the town and encroaching on these residential areas which were soon abandoned in favour of the leafy heights of Woodhouse and Headingley away from the industrial dirt.

Woodhouse Square, started 1830

Headingley Lane. Doorway c.1836

Blenheim Terrace. Doorway late 1830s

Gledhow Grove (now Chapel Allerton Hospital). Stable late 1830s by John Clark

Left. Roundhay Mansion c.1820 by John Clark. Portico

Meanwood Hall (now Meanwood Park Hospital) c.1830 by John Clark

Armley House c. 1829 by Sir Robert Smirke. (Wings now demolished)

Kirkstall or New Grange (Part of City of Leeds College of Education) 1725. Altered c. 1834 and c. 1858. Medallion in Entrance Hall

The late eighteenth century enthusiasm for the antiquities of ancient Greece led to the proliferation of Greek details on buildings. Sir Robert Smirke, the leading Greek Revivalist, designed Armley House c.1820 using the Ionic order, and most of the other large houses of the next decade were in the same noble, if slightly forbidding style. The stone version used in Leeds was very different from the light-hearted stucco of Cheltenham and Brighton. The interiors of the houses showed the same enthusiasm for the antique and the rooms had a cold, classical quality which was impressive although slightly monumental. The finest of these houses were designed by John Clark who was probably responsible for the whole group of mansions in Roundhay, Gledhow and Meanwood which show the change from the purely Greek to the mixed Greek-Italianate of the late 30's and the 40's. Many of the medium-sized houses in Woodhouse and Headingley followed the same fashion.

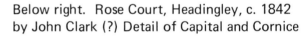

Roundhay Hall c.1830 by John Clark (?)
Staircase, Entrance Hall and Ceiling Detail

Below right. Rose Court, Headingley, c. 1842
by John Clark (?) Detail of Capital and Cornice

GREEK REVIVAL

Woodhouse Cemetery. Gatehouse 1835
by John Clark

eds Library, Commercial Street,
08 by Thomas Johnson

The pale yellow stucco of the elegant Leeds Library had no successors in the town. The other new buildings in a neat Regency Greek style were more soberly built of stone, but they formed a distinguished little group. R. D. Chantrell designed the Baths and the Philosophical Hall in 1819, followed in 1824 by his South Market which was an ambitious project with a circular Doric temple and two fountains.

Francis Goodwin designed the Central Market in 1824, and Samuel Chapman the Corn Exchange in 1826, but it was John Clark who added the most distinguished buildings to the early 19th century town when he designed the dignified Ionic Commercial Buildings in 1826 and later the circular Corinthian Yorkshire Bank on the opposite corner of Boar Lane. In 1834 he built the Leeds Savings Bank in Bond Street, and in 1835 Woodhouse Cemetery, a private burial ground with an Ionic mortuary chapel, a Doric gate-lodge and several noble Greek monuments.

Hope Foundry, Mabgate, c.1812

Central Market, Duncan Street, 1824 by Francis Goodwin (demolished).
From contemporary aquatint

Page 34. Woodhouse Cemetery. Memorial to Rev. R.W. Hamilton 1851 by J. Dobson

Exchange Buildings, Boar Lane, 1826 by John Clark (demolished).
Engraved by John Lucas from architect's drawing

GOTHIC REVIVAL

In 1818 the first Church Building Act set aside £1,000,000 which could be drawn upon by the Commissioners appointed to arrange for the building of new churches, particularly in the churchless areas in the expanding industrial towns. There was little money to spare on extravagant details and the term 'Commissioners' church' has been sneeringly applied to these buildings.

Although there was a battle between the Greeks and the Goths in some parishes, Leeds was wholeheartedly Gothic from the beginning. Out of the first grant three new churches were built between 1823 and 1825, Christ Church in Meadow Lane, St. Mary's, Quarry Hill and St. Mark's, Woodhouse. In a thinly decorated 18th century Gothic tradition this group had a quality lacking on the whole in the next group (11 in Leeds) built in the middle of the 19th century with the aid of a second grant. Each of the three held around 1,000 worshippers and cost about £10,000; it is no wonder that the Gothic detailing was sparingly applied.

St. Mark's Church, Woodhouse, 1823-25 by Atkinson and Sharpe

Below and Right. St. Mary's Church, Quarry Hill, 1823-25 by Thomas Taylor. East End and Tower

GOTHIC REVIVAL

CHRIST CHURCH, MEADOW LANE, 1823-25
Architect R. D. Chantrell

Above. Christ Church, Meadow Lane, 1823-25
by R.D. Chantrell. Detail of Ceiling
Left. St. George's Church 1836-38 by John Clark

In Christ Church, Chantrell produced not
only one of the best Commissioners' churches
but a surprisingly serious attempt at the Perpendicular style. He used cast-iron piers and so,
too, did Clark in his only non-Greek building
in Leeds—St. George's. It was in the thin lancet
window manner of Taylor's Yorkshire churches
but had an ambitiously pinnacled tower and spire
which were destroyed in a gale in 1962. The
churches in this group, and among them should
be included Taylor's St. John's, Roundhay and,
for its date, the curiously naive Holy Trinity,
Meanwood by W. Railton (better known as the
designer of the Nelson Column in Trafalgar
Square), were all very similar in plan and detailing. They were designed by men who had been
trained in the Classical tradition but were
turning to Gothic to meet a new demand. They
were not lacking in character even if they appear
starved by comparison with their successors.

GOTHIC REVIVAL AND NEO-NORMAN

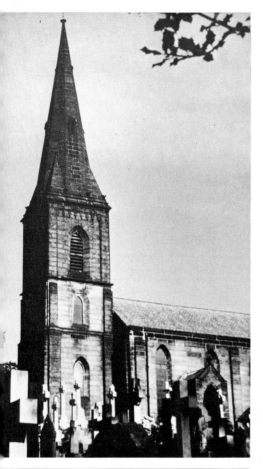

Above. Holy Trinity Church, Meanwood, 1849
by William Railton

Above left. St. John's Church, Roundhay, 1824-26
by Thomas Taylor

Left. St. Paul's Church, Shadwell, 1841-42
by R.D. Chantrell. A Neo-Norman example

GOTHIC REVIVAL

PARISH CHURCH OF ST. PETER 1839-41
Architect R. D. Chantrell

During his ten years as Vicar of Leeds the energetic Dr. Hook revitalised the Church in the town; having 'found it a stronghold of Dissent, he left it a stronghold of the Church.' As part of this work he demolished the old St. Peter's and commissioned Chantrell in 1839 to build a new Parish Church. Chantrell had already built Christ Church in the Perpendicular style but for the larger building he looked farther back, to the transitional period between the Decorated and the Perpendicular. This allowed him a flexibility in interpreting the Gothic details which later generations frowned on as unscholarly, and he built a church which seems now, in spite of some heaviness inside the building, the last assertion of 18th century Romanticism.

The centrally placed tower and the resulting axial plan in which the monumental organ case faced the main entrance were expressions of a Classical form of planning. The Gothic detailing of the tracery, doors and pinnacles was nearer to the work of James and Jeffry Wyatt at Fonthill and Ashridge than to the almost contemporary detailing by A. W. Pugin on the Houses of Parliament. The richly picturesque interior with its assortment of Baroque cartouche memorials from the old church, early Victorian stained glass and elaborate monuments to the leading townsmen has a touchingly human quality.

Page 40. Interior looking West

Above. Statue of St. Peter from organ case of Old Parish Church
Below. Tower and West End

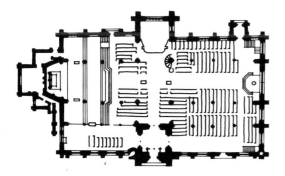

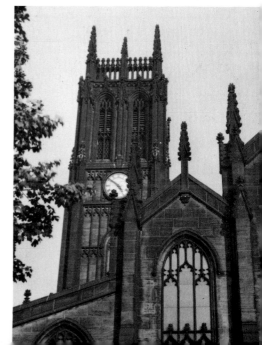

GOTHIC REVIVAL   ST. SAVIOUR'S CHURCH, ELLERBY ROAD

Dr. Hook's churchmanship was of the traditional school but during his vicariate the Oxford Movement, the Tractarianism of Newman and Pusey, was growing in strength. The form of the church began to assume greater importance as the minutiae of the ritual were endlessly discussed. Partly as an attempt to establish the principles of Tractarianism and partly to combat 'gross profligacy combined perhaps with attendance at socialistic meetings' the church of St. Saviour was built between 1842 and 1845 on a commanding site south-east of the Parish Church. It was designed by John Macduff Derick, an Irishman of few buildings, but it was never completed according to the original design. In spite of the generosity of Dr. Pusey himself there was insufficient money to build the ambitiously large, rich tower and spire.

The cruciform plan of the church (it was originally intended to dedicate it to the Holy Cross) with the traditional divisions of nave, chancel and transepts marked a serious return, not only to the older form of ritual, but also to a more scholarly interpretation of the older architecture. For this building the Decorated style was chosen; its seriousness, combined with the splendid glass designed by Pugin and William Morris and Co., contrasted forcibly with the conservatism of the Parish Church.

St. Saviour's 1842-45 by J.M. Derick

Above. Contemporary lithograph showing spire that was never built

Left. Nave and Chancel

Page 43. Window in South Transept designed by A.W.N. Pugin and made by Michael O'Connor

GOTHIC REVIVAL

Cobble Hall, Roundhay, c.1820

Cumberland Priory, Headingley, c. 1836

Ashwood House, Headingley Lane, c.1836

GOTHIC REVIVAL

eadingley Castle c.1840

The new interest in the Middle Ages, dating from the second half of the 18th century, had little effect in Leeds until the 19th but gradually the pointed arch or the Tudor hood-mould began to appear on houses. An early example on the Roundhay estate was a typical Georgian house with 'Gothic' windows and battlements on the outbuildings. In the late 30's and the 40's a number of Gothic houses were built in Headingley, some of them with battlements and turreted towers although none of the owners seems to have been enthusiastic enough to want a moat or drawbridge. Plainer Tudor or Jacobean houses were more popular than the extravagantly Gothic, possibly because they could be built more cheaply. Although some of them looked picturesquely irregular from the outside most of these houses were not very different inside from the traditional Georgian pattern and few had medieval interiors.

Below, Left and Right. North Hill House, Headingley, c.1860. Detail over Door and Entrance Front

Roundhay Park. Castle 1821

Above right. Bear Pit, Cardigan Road, 1840

Weetwood Hall. Grotto c.1870

The 18th and 19th century Romantics who delighted in building Gothic or neo-Tudor houses found an easier outlet for their enthusiasm in structures not intended for habitation (although occasionally a hermit was encouraged to take up residence.) A mock ruin, such as the one in the woods at the end of the Waterloo Lake on the Roundhay estate, or 'King Alfred's Castle' which until recently stood in Stonegate Road, was built as part of the designed landscape around a large house. Such a building usually served no useful purpose—a true folly—but when the Leeds Zoological and Botanical Gardens were opened in 1840 the captive bears were exhibited in a large circular pit behind a castellated facade; the animals were safely behind a portcullis and were viewed from the top of one of the turrets.

Another form of diversion in the landscape was a grotto, usually set in a thickly wooded part of the estate and approached between high rocks to induce a melancholy delight or horror. Such a sensation was modified in the 19th century when the grotto was more often joined to the house but the example at Weetwood Hall might recall Dr. Johnson's comment that 'a grotto is a very pleasant place—for a toad.'

NONCONFORMISM

The Nonconformists developed a plain form of meeting-house in which to worship according to their beliefs but the growing number of sects and their adherents resulted in larger and consequently more imposing buildings to accommodate as many people as possible. The exteriors, such as Brunswick Chapel, were generally neatly but sparsely Classical on the fronts and plain at the sides. The interiors too were puritanically severe but in 1827 an organ in a richly carved case was installed in Brunswick Chapel. Regarded by the stricter Dissenters as 'not so much a desire to increase holy and hallowing influence upon the hearts and lives of the congregation, as to please the ear and captivate the passions', it caused dissension among the Methodists and the formation of yet another sect, the Protestant Methodists. In 1841 the new Congregational Chapel in East Parade appeared in a strict Doric order, departing from the simplicity of the earlier meeting-houses but remaining aloof from the revived Gothic of the established church. In 1848 *The Ecclesiologist* was shocked to report 'The Unitarians of Leeds, *horribile dictu*, are building a meeting-house in florid Middle Pointed'; Mill Hill Chapel marked the beginning of the capitulation of Nonconformism to the pointed arch. The smaller chapels and the temperance halls, such as that at Woodhouse, continued for a time to be built in a simple Georgian tradition but even Cuthbert Brodrick turned to the Gothic when he designed Headingley Hill Chapel. Only the Quakers were unconvinced and when the new Friends' Meeting House was built in 1866 it was in a sober grey Italianate dress.

Brunswick Chapel 1825 by J. Simpson
From an engraving by J.N. Bean

Brunswick Chapel. Organ Case 1827

Mill Hill Chapel 1848
by Bowman and Crowther

East Parade Chapel 1841 by Moffat and Hurst
(demolished)

Woodhouse Temperance Hall,
Institution Street, 1850

Friends' Meeting House, Woodhouse Lane,
by E. Birchall (now B.B.C.)

ROMAN CATHOLICISM

ount St. Mary's, Church Road, 1852
y Joseph Hansom
hancel and transepts added 1866 by
W. Pugin

The Roman Catholic churches which were built after the Relief Act of 1791 were faithful to the pre-Reformation pointed arch. A. W. Pugin designed the reredos (1842) in the first St. Anne's Cathedral but the finest of the mid-19th century Roman churches was Hansom's Mount St. Mary's.

Below. Warehouses east of Leeds Bridge (demolished)

Above. Terminal of Aire and Calder Navigation, Dock Street, c.1830

Warehouses and factories changed slowly in design, owing a little to the current fashions but absorbing them into the vernacular rather than being dictated by them. These simple strong buildings had a dignity which more self-consciously monumental buildings often failed to achieve and the best of those on the Aire had this quality. It is a characteristic which is peculiarly associated with waterways; the similar quality of the buildings of the canal authorities is also seen in the detailing of the lock gates, bridges and railings which are firmly in the functional tradition. Many of these buildings were erected in the 18th century but they continued to be built in the 19th and provided a sober dignified background to the occasional architectural follies such as Temple Mills or Tower Works. There was a fine quality in the simple but massive detailing of the best of these buildings.

INDUSTRIAL

TEMPLE MILLS, MARSHALL STREET, 1838
Architect Ignatius Bonomi

Page 52. Facade to Marshall Street

Interior from engraving 1843

Detail of Facade

One of the best-known exceptions to the rule of simple functional buildings for industry was Temple Mills. Italianate designs were not unusual in the West Riding but this flax-spinning mill is probably unique; Ignatius Bonomi (from Durham despite his name) designed the building in 1838 in an Egyptian temple style with battered walls, papyrus and lotus flower capitals, and winged solar discs in the huge coved cornice, all based closely on the two thousand years old temple at Edfu. Probably the influence of the architect's brother, Joseph, a noted Egyptologist, was responsible for the choice of style but the interior was rationally designed to obtain an even illumination over the workroom floor through 66 glass domes; the only Egyptian details inside were the capitals of the cast-iron columns.

Above. Medallion of Josue Heilmann by Alfred Drury

Right. 'Giotto' Chimney 1899 by William Bakewell

In 1857 '*The Builder*' published a complaint from Mr. P. Rawlinson that 'a first vision of British chimneys, as contemplated from our railways, must have caused a nightmare to sensitive foreigners' and an illustration showing the writer's vision of a group of Italian towers adapted as chimneys. A few years later the visitor approaching Leeds by rail could see a new chimney, part of Tower Works, based on the great Lamberti tower in Verona and modified for its more prosaic use by Thomas Shaw in 1864. This first echo of Italy was completely overshadowed at the end of the century by the huge copy of Giotto's marble campanile in Florence, built as a second chimney in the same factory: the red brick tower, which has gilded tiled panels behind the traceried 'bell-louvres', was ingeniously made to form part of a dust extraction plant in the industrial process. The boiler house was designed at its base as a tribute to famous textile engineers, and its white-tiled walls were decorated with large portrait medallions by Alfred Drury.

CLASSICAL

TOWN HALL 1853-58
Architect Cuthbert Brodrick

In 1850 the idea of building a Town Hall was first proposed and it became the greatest local issue of the decade. This was the opportunity for the growing town to assert itself and to build a memorial to its own success and pride; it was also the chance for those who believed that 'if a noble municipal palace that might vie with some of the best Town Halls of the Continent were to be erected in the middle of their hitherto squalid and unbeautiful town, it would become a practical admonition to the populace of the value of beauty and art, and in course of time men would learn to live up to it.' A competition was held in 1852 and the first prize was awarded to Cuthbert Brodrick, a young Hull architect who was unknown outside his native town. The foundation stone was laid in August 1853 but the design was revised many times during the construction of the building; the inclusion of a tower was debated as great length but finally civic pride in the great new buildings which were expected to be 'famous beyond their own limits, and, like the noble halls of France, of Belgium and of Italy . . . to attract . . . dilettante tourists, and the lovers of art from distant places' won the battle. The Town Hall was more than a building; the words of the choral exhortation sung at the foundation-stone laying ceremony expressed its symbolism:

'*May the Hall whose foundations thus broadly are laid*
Stand a trophy to Freedom—to Peace and to Trade.'

It was opened by Queen Victoria on 7th September 1858 although the work was not finally completed until 1860 when the great bell, bearing on one side the royal profile, was hung in the tower.

Above. View from the Headrow

Below. Doorway in facade to Oxford Place

CLASSICAL

TOWN HALL 1853-58
Organ Case and Detail of Victoria Hall

The moral virtues were emphasised in the richly decorated Victoria Hall by the painting of improving mottoes along the frieze and round the arch of the organ apse. The sculptured tympanum by John Thomas over the main entrance showed an allegory of Leeds encouraging commerce and industry and fostering the arts and sciences. All the wealth of mid-Victorian craftsmanship was lavished on the building; John Crace, the fashionable London decorator, designed and executed the painted decorations; richly coloured glass by James Hartley of Manchester, cut-glass chandeliers by Osler's of Birmingham, and prismatic lanterns by Defries of London added to the brilliance; the floor of the entrance vestibule was paved with Minton tiles, and the apse at the end of the hall was filled with a mammoth organ case. Everything was of the best and in this, his finest building, Brodrick revitalised the languishing Classical tradition (or led it to a grand close), by expressing in monumental stone the spirit of mid-Victorian provincial pride and confidence.

Brodrick built up a practice in Leeds on the success of the Town Hall and he was regarded as one of the leading architects in the country. He was invited to submit schemes for important buildings in London and abroad, but he built little outside Yorkshire and his best work is in Leeds.

Plan.
Upper half
as designed;
lower half
as built

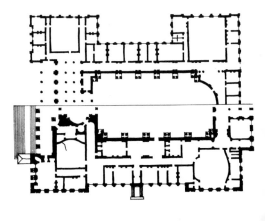

CLASSICAL

TOWN HALL 1853-58
Engraving of Victoria Hall 1858 by Orlando Jewett

CLASSICAL

CORN EXCHANGE 1861
Architect Cuthbert Brodrick

In 1860 Brodrick won the competition for the new Corn Exchange, a great elliptical domed building which was an exercise in the use of the curve. Walls, arches, porches and steps were all curved in this monument to the corn trade. The building was faced with diamond-rusticated masonry, an unusual detail which was taken from the Romantic Classical buildings of 19th century France which Brodrick greatly admired, and the detailing of the masonry was executed with his characteristic vigour.

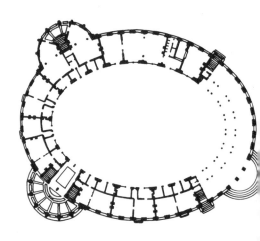

CLASSICAL

CORN EXCHANGE 1861
Architect Cuthbert Brodrick

Details of
Facade

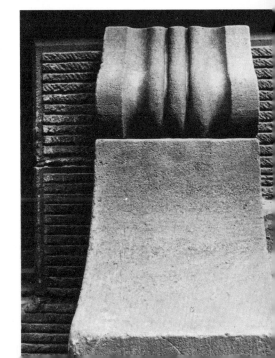

CLASSICAL

CORN EXCHANGE 1861
Architect Cuthbert Brodrick

BATHS

CLASSICAL

MECHANICS' INSTITUTE 1865
Architect Cuthbert Brodrick

Architect's Original Drawing

Right. Detail of Plinth

The third of Brodrick's civic buildings was the Mechanics' Institute which he designed in 1865. The influence of Second Empire French architecture can be seen more strongly than in any of his other buildings in Leeds. His enthusiasm for France, which was shared by other architects who had seen much to admire at the Paris Exhibition ten years earlier, found its finest expression in the Grand Hotel at Scarborough but it was apparent in the pavilion roof, the steeply battered basement and the huge central arch of the Institute.

Opposite the Mechanics' Institute, Brodrick built in 1866 the Oriental Baths with crowning domes and minarets. The building was refaced in 1882 but the coloured brickwork which he had used, and the moulded brickwork on his group of warehouses in King Street, became common in external decoration, combined with encaustic tiles and terra cotta. His assistant, William Hill, designed the offices of the Poor Law Guardians in East Parade (1859) and the old Dispensary in New Briggate (1865) in a heavy Italianate manner but the only Classical buildings of the mid-century which can rank with Brodrick's are the palatial, Venetian Renaissance office of the Leeds and Yorkshire Assurance Company in Albion Street, the nearby Leeds Club, and the Bank of England in South Parade.

Oriental Baths, Cookridge Street, 1866 by Cuthbert Brodrick. Altered 1882 (demolished). From the architect's water colour drawing

Warehouse Doorway, King Street, 186? by Cuthbert Brodrick (demolished)

Above. Leeds Club, Albion Place.
Facade altered 1863
Left. Leeds and Yorkshire Assurance
Company's Office (now Leek and
Westbourne Building Society),
Commercial Street, 1852-55
by W.B. Gingell
Below. Bank of England, South Parade,
1862-64 by Philip Hardwick

Armley Prison 1847 by Perkin and Backhouse.
Enlarged 1857
From Lithograph 1846 by S.O. Bailey

It was probably an association with the medieval tradition of captivity in castle dungeons that suggested the form of Armley Prison. The castellated style had already reached its climax in the late 20's with the rebuilding of Windsor Castle for George IV but it continued to be thought of as a symbolically penitential style eminently suitable for prisons.

Prison Gatehouse

GOTHIC REVIVAL   **LEEDS GRAMMAR SCHOOL**

Leeds Grammar School 1857 by E.M. Barry
From the architect's water colour drawing

It was not surprising that E. M. Barry, the son of the architect of the Houses of Parliament, chose the Gothic style for the new Grammar School buildings. Dr. Arnold at Rugby had strengthened the adherence to the monastic and literary conception of education which went back to the Middle Ages; he had set up the ideal of the Christian Gentleman as the product of the English public school and only one style of architecture could be considered appropriate to match this ideal—Gothic.

School Chapel 1862-63 by E.M. Barry

GOTHIC REVIVAL

GENERAL INFIRMARY, 1862-68
Architect Sir George Gilbert Scott

'If Gilbert Scott will undertake the plan he will do it well.' The Infirmary Building Committee took this advice and appointed Scott to design their new building in 1862. He had already built a splendid Gothic bank in Park Row (demolished 1964) and when asked about the appropriateness of a Gothic Infirmary he had given his opinion that 'some form of Architecture founded on the Medieval styles but freely treated would meet the requirements of such a building better than any other style.' The exterior had distinct echoes of the hotel at St. Pancras which, as well as the Albert Memorial, Scott was designing at this time. The 'pavilion' plan which provided cross-lighting and ventilation in the wards was adopted on Florence Nightingale's advice and across the centre of the building was a cast-iron and glass Winter Garden. The plan was acclaimed as 'perfect . . . calculated to place it in the foremost rank of European Hospitals'.

Beckett's Bank (later Westminster), Park Row 1862 by Sir G.G. Scott (demolished)

Photograph c.1895 from South West
Page 67. Portico on South Facade

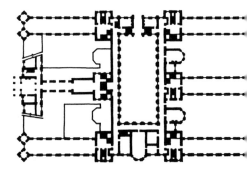

GOTHIC REVIVAL

Perhaps Scott's use of the Gothic style for the Infirmary helped to establish it in Leeds. The builder of the shops opposite copied his window details, and nearby offices and a public house were given pointed arches and foliated capitals. A few hundred yards away the Masonic Hall was loosely modelled externally on a Venetian Gothic palazzo and its main room was surrounded by an arcade with clustered shafts and carved capitals. Few architects followed completely Ruskin's advocacy of the 14th century Venetian Gothic as the only possible style but many took to heart his advice never to imitate anything but natural forms. Capitals and bases of columns, panels in gables and window spandrels, porches over doorways, all were decorated with leaves, birds, animals and flowers. The holly and the ivy, the honeysuckle and the bee, were realistically carved in stone on offices and town halls, railway stations, gin palaces and public lavatories. The skill employed was often beyond criticism and the enthusiasm was genuine but, by the time the naturalistic carvings were appearing on the new buildings in Leeds, Ruskin was having doubts about the result of his advice since 'sometimes behind an engine furnace, or a railroad bank, you may detect the pathetic discord of a Gothic capital's momentary grace and, with toil, decipher its floral carvings choked with soot'.

The most notable eclectic Gothic buildings in the town were designed by a Scotsman, George Corson, who set up practice in 1859. His first important building, Hepper House (1863) showed his predilection for elaborately carved natural forms in the decoration and his use of a mixture of stylistic sources. Romanesque and Byzantine, French and English Gothic, were all adapted in a vigorous fashion. In the Sun Life Assurance Company's building, he demonstrated his mastery of the round arch and his use of lavishly carved capitals.

Hepper House, East Parade, 1863 by George Corson

Victoria Hotel, Great George Street c. 1867

Above. Old Masonic Hall, Great George Street, 1866 by Perkin and Sons
Left. Britannia Buildings, Oxford Place, c. 1868
Below left. 44 Park Place, 1870 by George Corson
Below. Sun Buildings, Park Row, 1877 by George Corson (demolished)

Details of Sculpture on Balustrade
and Staircase

Municipal Buildings 1878-84 by George Corson.
Detail of Facade

Scottish Widows' Assurance Society,
Park Row, 1869 by George Corson

Hyde Gardens, Clarendon Road,
1868 by George Corson
(now Cornhill House)

Corson even used the Renaissance style occasionally; he designed the Municipal Buildings (1876-84) and the School Board Office (1878-81) in a French-Italian mixed Renaissance style to harmonise with Brodrick's Town Hall, and the Scottish Widows' Assurance Company's building (1869) to harmonise with Hardwick's Bank of England (1862-4). Inside the Municipal Buildings, however, he used a mixture of Romanesque and Byzantine with strongly naturalistic, carved decoration.

He built offices and warehouses, sometimes using Gothic porches reminiscent of Venice and Verona, and sometimes turrets and heavy plain masonry details suggestive of his native Scotland. He set a pattern of dignified, lavishly stylistic commercial buildings which was followed by other architects in Leeds, helping to give a feeling of architectural richness to the business centre of the town.

GRAND THEATRE 1878

In 1859 there was a meeting to discuss the need for a new theatre in Leeds; when it was at last built by Corson almost 20 years later it was given a Romantic exterior with Romanesque windows, turrets and allegorical figures on foliated brackets. The oddly ecclesiastical effect was not altogether dissipated in the richly decorated auditorium with its swaying balcony fronts, fan-vaulted spandrels, rose-window ceiling, and a proscenium arch like a set of mammoth organ-pipes. All the surfaces were encrusted with elaborate plaster and papier-maché gilded decoration, as eclectic as usual in Corson's work and suggesting that he had taken a long look at Owen Jones's influential 'Grammar of Ornament.' As well as this outstanding example of theatre architecture there is the famous Palace of Varieties. Its mid-19th century auditorium was conservatively in the tradition of the preceding century when the theatre was first built.

Grand Theatre. Facade. Engraving of first design.
Page 72. Grand Theatre. Detail of Interior
Below. City Palace of Varieties. Auditorium c.1850

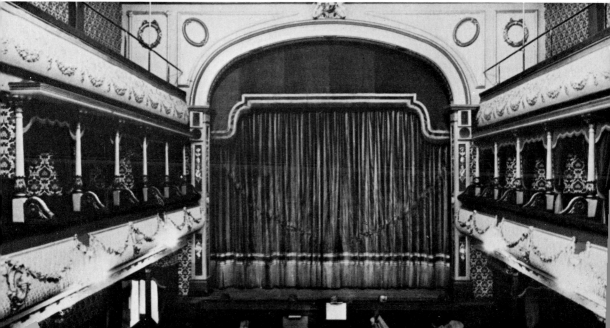

Above, Right and Left. Turk's Head (Whitelock's), Briggate, late 19th Century
Left. Pack Horse Hotel, Woodhouse Lane. Carved Keystone mid 19th Century

In the 18th and 19th centuries every second building in the courtyards and alleys off Briggate seems to have been a tavern dating from the time when the cloth market was held in the street after moving away from the old Leeds Bridge. Relics of several are still left, but the most famous and least altered is Whitelock's Turk's Head tavern, its narrow entrance court leading into the long, low room which is artlessly filled with twisted brass columns, mirrors, polychromatic tiling and Victorian lettering.

GOTHIC REVIVAL

Above. Thornton's Arcade, Briggate, 1878

Above left. Gaumont Cinema (originally Coliseum), Cookridge Street, 1885 by W. Bakewell

For the rest of the century the Gothic, increasingly eclectic in its interpretation, was the most widely used style for banks, offices and warehouses. Brodrick's Oriental Baths were Gothicised in 1882 when the facade was decorated with a swimmer determinedly diving out of a Gothic canopied niche. Thornton's Arcade (1878) was completely Gothic in its detailing and so were the Church Institute (1866-8), the Fire Station (1883) and the Coliseum (1885). Thomas Ambler added an exotic building to the town in 1878 when he built a Moorish-Venetian warehouse in St. Pauls Street. He was a prolific designer, remarkably varied in his use of the mixed-Gothic and the Renaissance, but his most surprising design was the completely cast-iron and glass facade of a warehouse in Basinghall Street (1873).

Public Baths, Cookridge Street, refaced 1882 (demolished)

ST. PAUL'S HOUSE, PARK SQUARE, 1878
Architect Thomas Ambler

Left.
St. Paul's
House.
Terra cotta
decoration

Right.
Warehouse,
Basinghall
Street.
1873 by
Thomas Ambler.
Lithograph
1875

Left.
St. Paul's
House.
Terra cotta
decoration

Right.
30 Park Place
c.1870 by
Thomas Ambler

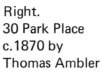

Above. Meanwood Towers 1867 by E. W. Pugin
Above left. Cookridge Convalescent Hospital.
Lodge 1868 by Norman Shaw
Centre left. Alder Hill, Meanwood, c.1870

In the 60's architects had a wide choice of medieval details and a richly varied selection of building materials. E. W. Pugin built Meanwood Towers in 1867 using gables, ornamental chimney stacks and oriel windows in an abandoned profusion. The following year Norman Shaw designed Cookridge Convalescent Hospital in a more restrained manner but it was in the tradition of Sussex, not Yorkshire. Although E. S. Prior made a sensitive design for Carr Manor in 1881 in the Yorkshire manor-house tradition most architects and builders were content to use any details and materials which made their houses picturesque. Buildings such as Cookridge Hospital and Alder Hill, Meanwood, led on to the large half-timbered houses in Roundhay and the smaller versions, detached or semi-detached, in every residential suburb.

Carr Manor, Meanwood, 1881 by E. S. Prior

SPENFIELD, OTLEY ROAD
Architect George Corson

ntrance Doorway

etail of Capitals in Entrance Hall

Above. Additional decoration in Drawing Room 1888 by J. F. Armitage

Spenfield 1875-76, enlarged 1890

George Corson made his usual individual contribution, designing several large houses in Headingley which were chunkily picturesque and slightly forbidding. His own house, Dunearn (1882) had gables, dormer windows and projecting bays but there was nothing pretty about the result. Some of his other designs, such as Spenfield (1875-6), were externally severe but richly decorated inside. Spenfield is the domestic equivalent of the Grand Theatre, filled with marble shafted columns, stained glass, ornate brasswork and elaborate plasterwork in swirling relief on the ceilings and friezes. The drawing-room was redecorated in 1888 by J. F. Armitage in a fashionable 'Peacock' manner.

TEMPLENEWSAM

Above. Dining Room 1894 by C.E. Kempe

Page 80 and Left. Oak Staircase 1894 by C.E. Kempe

The final alterations to Templenewsam were made in 1894 when C. E. Kempe built the oak staircase, copying it from the Jacobean design at Slaugham Place, Sussex; at the same time he made the neo-Jacobean dining-room. But such historical accuracy was rare at the end of the century when houses were being more freely designed, under the influence of the Arts and Crafts Movement, in a new version of traditional (but not necessarily regional) domestic building.

Above.
The Great Hall
1877 and later
buildings

Staircase to
Great Hall
1877

Left.
Tower and
Clothworkers'
Court

THE UNIVERSITY

Above. Gable of Clothworkers' Court 1877 by Alfred Waterhouse

Left. School of Medicine 1894 by W. H. Thorpe

A new version of the old style was first seen in Leeds in 1877 when Alfred Waterhouse began to build the hot-coloured terra cotta and brick buildings of the Yorkshire College which became the nucleus of the University when it was founded in 1904. It was added to in a similar style (one which earned the architect the name of 'Slaughterhouse' because of his favourite red materials) in 1894 and by his son in 1898-1908.

The staircase leading to the Great Hall was lavishly faced with the faience tiling which was the speciality of the local Burmantofts factory, a form of decoration which was found ideal for their buildings by Waterhouse and his followers at the end of the century.

There is more Burmantofts tiling in the School of Medicine, a distinguished Gothic— Arts and Crafts design which replaced Corson's 30-year old building in Park Street.

Much of the late 19th century architecture was highly coloured in every sense; red brick, orange terra cotta and yellow faience were used in wildly free versions of English Jacobean, French or Italian Renaissance, or a mixture of all three. Waterhouse's characteristically hot colours were used on his bank for William Williams Brown and Co. (now Lloyds) in Park Row, but his offices for the Prudential Assurance Company were more delicately coloured. The Yorkshire Post building by Chorley and Connon was in-influenced by Waterhouse, but the same architects made an eclectic selection of details to incorporate in the terra cotta Liberal Club and Metropole Hotel. The Gothic style was still used, in a free way, as in the monumental Yorkshire Bank in Infirmary Street but the Classical (was it survival or revival?) was there too as in the Midland Bank, City Square by W. W. Gwyther, 1899. Architecture had many faces at the end of the century.

Above left. Detail of 'Yorkshire Post' Building, Albion Street, 1886-87 by Chorley and Connon

Below left. Detail of Yorkshire Bank Infirmary Street 1894 by Perkin and Bulmer

Below. Detail of Prudential Assurance Offices, Park Row, 1894 by Alfred Waterhouse

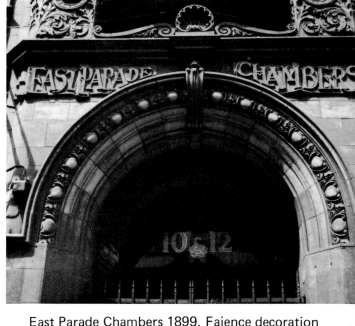

6 Park Place c.1895. Detail of terra cotta facing

East Parade Chambers 1899. Faience decoration

Detail of Lloyds Bank (originally William Williams, Brown and Co.), Park Row, 1898 by Alfred Waterhouse

Midland Bank (originally Yorkshire Banking Company), City Square, 1899 by W.W. Gwyther

GOTHIC REVIVAL **ST. CLEMENT'S CHURCH, SHEEPSCAR, 1868**
Architect George Corson

It is wrong to think of the 19th century churches as copies of the medieval; although the various church movements advocated the adoption of one or another plan form or style there was room for individuality. Scott was the greatest provider of churches, reliable, moderate (ecclesiologically speaking), buildings such as All Soul's, Blackman Lane. Lord Grimthorpe, well-known as an eminent litigator and clock-designer (and for his architectural omniscience), endowed St. Chad's, Headingley, which has sometimes been considered his own design; the architect was probably W. H. Crossland. These two churches can be taken as representative of conformist design of the 60's and 70's but Corson was unable to subdue his individuality and in St. Clement's, Sheepscar, he designed an impressive tower and a finely handled interior in which brick, stone and plaster were used as a setting for rich stone-carvings. Another individual design with great dramatic quality is Walker and Athron's St. Bartholomew's, Armley.

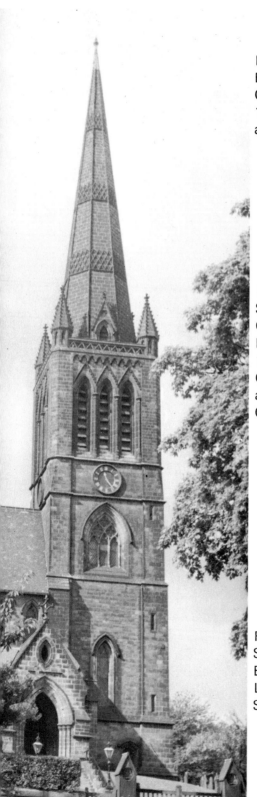

Right. St. Bartholomew's Church, Armley, 1872 by Walker and Athron.

Left. St. Chad's Church, Far Headingley, 1868 by Lord Grimthorpe and W.H. Crossland

Right. All Soul's Church, Blackman Lane, 1876 by Sir G. G. Scott

GOTHIC REVIVAL

ST. MICHAEL'S CHURCH, HEADINGLEY, 1884-90
Architect J.L. Pearson

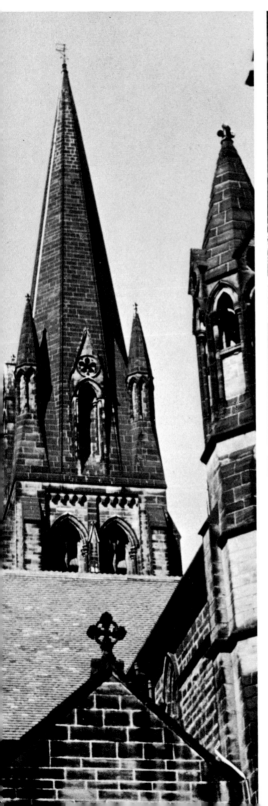

The work of Pearson and Bodley brought the 19th century Gothic Revival to a calmly triumphant conclusion. St. Michael's, Headingley, with its tall tower and impressive massing, has a spacious interior enriched by Pearson's iron screen and Temple Moore's reredos. In St. Matthew's, Chapel Allerton, the strong vertical lines of Bodley's refined Gothic are immediately recognisable and so is the use internally of subtle colour and low relief carving. In St. Edward's, Holbeck, the arcade was so far refined as to become a series of elegantly extruded arches; the vigour of the earlier 19th century Gothic was replaced by a subtle, almost sweet, simplicity.

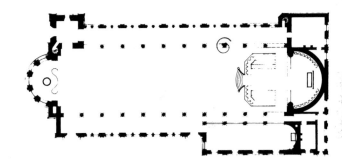

Occasionally the Gothic precedent was by-passed, as when St. Aidan's was designed by R. J. Johnson and Crawford - Hick in the form of a Romanesque basilica with apses at the east and west ends. The sumptuous effect of the richly decorated rood screen, capitals, pulpit and font was heightened in 1916 when the wall of the eastern apse was covered with a mosaic by Sir Frank Brangwyn.

Above. St. Aidan's Church, Roundhay Road, 1891-94 by R. J. Johnson and A. Crawford-Hick. Detail of Pulpit and Plan

Left. St. Matthew's Church, Chapel Allerton, 1897-98 by G. F. Bodley

ST. AIDAN'S CHURCH, ROUNDHAY ROAD,1891-94
Architect R.J. Johnson and A. Crawford-Hick

Above. St. Edward's Church, Holbeck, 1903-4 by G. F. Bodley. Reredos

Above left. Priory of St. Wilfrid, Springfield Mount, started 1902 by Temple Moore

Left. St. Anne's Cathedral, Cookridge Street, 1902-4 by S. K. Greenslade and J. H. Eastwood

As well as Bodley, other architects at the turn of the century were working in a medieval manner modified by the Arts and Crafts Movement. The detailing of St. Anne's Cathedral and the Priory of St. Wilfrid was in a medieval tradition rather than in a particular style, often beautiful but lacking the vigour and inventiveness of the best of the 19th century Gothic.

COUNTY ARCADE 1898-1900
Architect F. Matcham

The County Arcade, a palace for shoppers was completed at the beginning of the century when a large area between Vicar Lane and Briggate, including the commemoratively named Queen Victoria and King Edward Streets, was developed to an overall plan and a uniform red and orange facade lavishly decorated with gables, corner towers and 'mixed' architectural trimmings. It was designed by an architect who had been responsible for over 100 theatres and musichalls, including the London Coliseum and Palladium, and the development included the gaudy Empire Music Hall and the King Edward Restaurant which was richly furnished with a Mexican onyx and marble staircase, mosaic floors, polished marble walls and columns in 'the handsomest Grill Room in the United Kingdom'; statues of the Venus de Medici and the Venus de Milo and paintings by eminent Royal Academicians showed that culture was not forgotten in this riot of richness. Running through the length of one of the buildings is the County Arcade, still complete in its finery of marble pilasters with gilded capitals, mosaic spandrels under the dome and exuberant wrought iron gates and grilles.

An historical style had very often been qualified as 'freely treated', an apt description of the City Market which welded Venetian Baroque domes, medieval towers from the Low Countries, panels of Art Nouveau decoration and other richly diverse details into one glorious salute to the new century. Inside the building cast-iron dragons hold up a gallery, and Classical cast-iron columns rise to support an octagonal dome beneath which formerly stood a cast-iron clock tower.

Details of County Arcade 1898-1900
by F. Matcham

CITY MARKETS 1903-4
Architects Leeming and Leeming

ART NOUVEAU

Above.
34 Wellington Street. Details of Railings c.1900

Left.
Morn, City Square, 1903 by Alfred Drury

Page 94. Below Right.
Clock from Central Octagon (now at Oakwood)

Art Nouveau, an attempt to abandon altogether the historical styles, was perhaps too precious and sophisticated to be adopted completely in the north of England but there are some surprisingly curvaceous railings in Wellington Street —as well as Alfred Drury's electric-torch-bearing nymphs in City Square; sculptured and moulded decoration on several buildings dating from the end of the century showed an increasing interest in flowing lines and free shapes, and the interiors of many buildings were decorated with woodwork and glass which was strongly influenced by the ideas of Art Nouveau.

Seacroft Hospital 1903 by E.T. Hall

Above. College of Art, Cookridge Street, 1903 by Bedford and Kitson. Mosaic by Gerald Moira

In the 80's the popularity of the so-called 'Queen Anne' style re-introduced a simpler approach to architecture; comparatively plain brickwork and white painted sash windows were used in Board schools, hospitals and offices. About the same time the Arts and Crafts Movement was leading a reaction against 19th century vulgarity and pomposity, encouraging a simpler form of design and a re-assessment of traditional building materials. These were the most important influences on early 20th century architecture. In such buildings as Seacroft Hospital, the College of Art and the Firemen's flats in Park Street could be seen the saner, if less superficially exciting, approach to design between 1900 and 1914. In them, in spite of the use of traditional materials and even Classical mouldings, the great changes on the way were clearly forecast.

Firemen's Flats, Park Street, 1909 by Percy Robinson

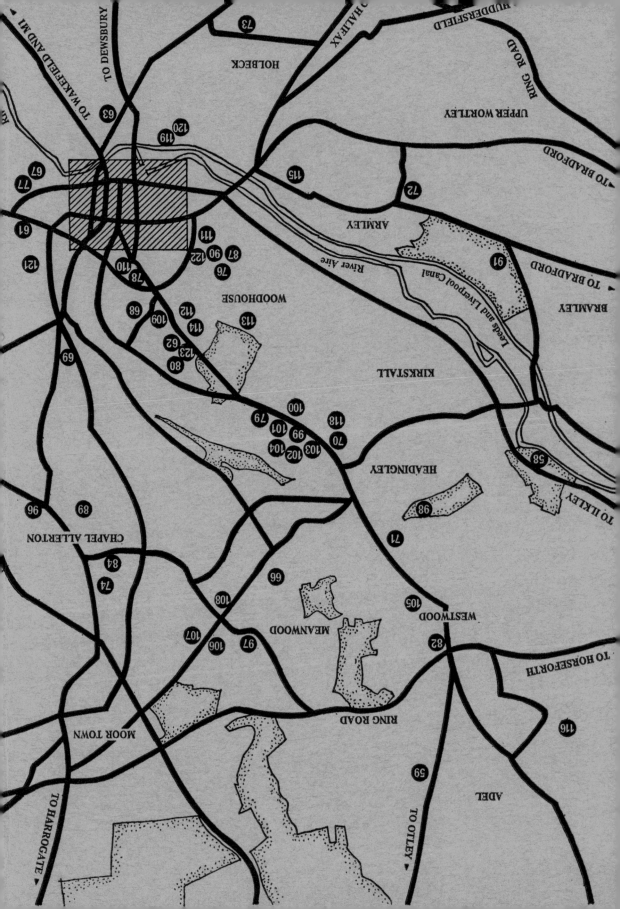